W0099654

Galileo Galilei

Charles Browne and Rob Waring

Series Editor **Rob Waring**

Level 3 - ⑤

Galileo Galilei

Charles Browne and Rob Waring

Series Editor: Rob Waring
Acquisitions Editor: Liana Robinson
Copy Editor: Casey Malarcher
Cover/Interior Design: Andy Roh

ISBN: 978-1-9464-5228-3

10 9 8 7 6 5 4 3 2 1
21 20 19 18 17

Contents

Early Life

Although Galileo was born in Italy more than 450 years ago, his influence on our lives even today is nothing short of amazing.

Have you ever used a thermometer when you were sick? Have you ever gone camping or hiking and used a compass to help you find your way? Do you like looking at the moon, stars, and planets at night using a telescope? These are just a few of the wonderful contributions Galileo gave to us.

Galileo's telescope was used to discover Jupiter's moons.

Galileo made many advances in the compass.

The Leaning Tower of Pisa, Italy

Galileo was born in 1564 in the famous town of Pisa during the time of the Italian Renaissance.

He was from a very large family and had five brothers and sisters.

Galileo had many brothers and sisters.

5

His father was a well-known musician and music teacher, and Galileo became very good at playing the lute from a very young age.

It is thought that his love and deep understanding of music later helped him to develop a mathematical mind with such precise thinking.

Galileo's ability in music is said to have helped him in math and science.

A portrait of Galileo Galilei

The church of Santa Maria Novella in Florence, Italy

Modern Florence

When Galileo was 10 years old, his family moved to the city of Florence. And when he was old enough, he began studying at a monastery.

Although his father wanted him to become a doctor, he much preferred the study of math and physics. Eventually, he convinced his father to let him focus on math.

Medieval doctors

The Young Scientist

Galileo's first experiments were with balls, levers, weights, and other objects. He observed everything and carefully recorded what happened.

Early experiments

This way of researching things was very unusual because in Galileo's time there were not scientists like we have today. Until that time, people just studied the works of classic philosophers and accepted those ideas to be true. Galileo's experiments and discoveries challenged many traditional beliefs.

Galileo's astronomical observatory in Padova, Italy

One of the first things he experimented with was a lamp hanging from the ceiling of a church. He noticed that no matter how far the lamp swung in one direction, it took exactly the same amount of time to swing back. This discovery eventually led to the invention of the pendulum clock.

A church lamp

9

The Leaning Tower of Pisa

Another famous story about Galileo has to do with the Leaning Tower of Pisa. In Galileo's time, most people believed that objects of different weights would fall at different speeds, with heavier ones falling faster than lighter ones.

Galileo challenged this belief by doing experiments where he dropped balls of different weights from the top of the Tower of Pisa. He showed that they fell at the same speed and landed at the same time!

A New Method

Galileo's careful methods were ahead of their time and set the stage for the scientific era.

Today, scientists study things using something called "the scientific method." What they do is identify a problem and then gather a lot of information and data about the problem. Next they come up with some ideas based on the data and then test to see if those ideas are correct. These methods and procedures are all based on the work of Galileo.

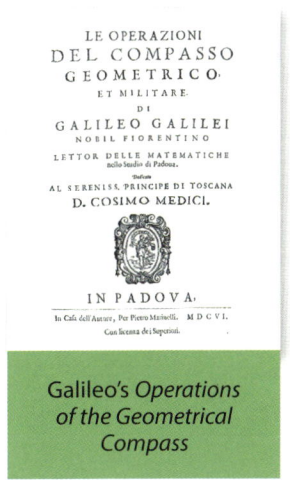

Galileo's *Operations of the Geometrical Compass*

Basic steps of the scientific method

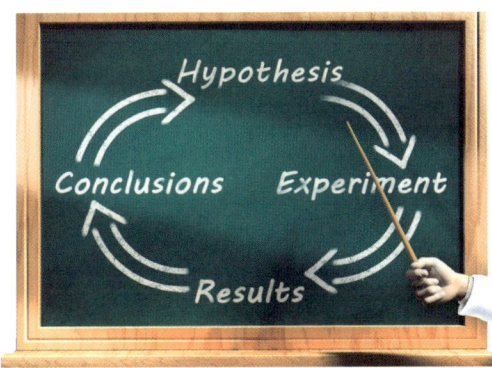

The Earth Goes Around the Sun

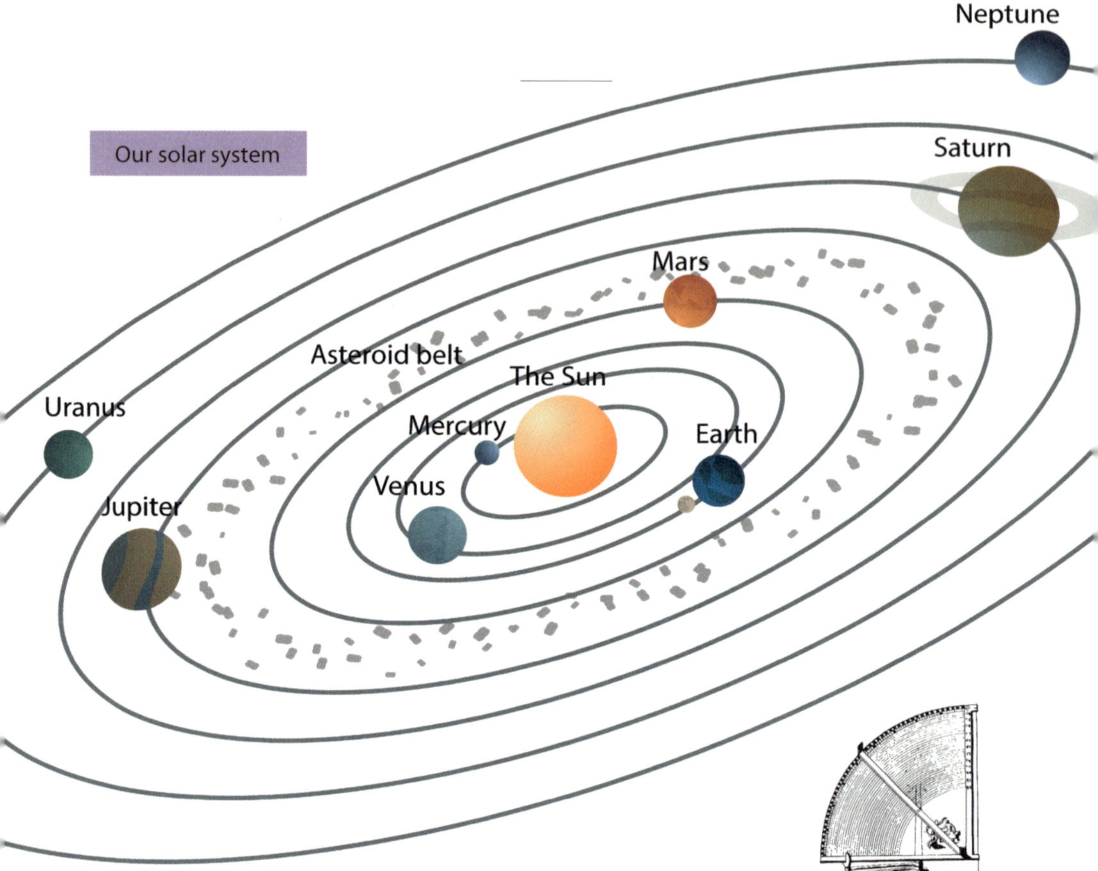

Neptune

Saturn

Mars

Asteroid belt

The Sun

Uranus

Mercury

Earth

Venus

Jupiter

An astrolabe

An ancient instrument for understanding the stars

In the time of Galileo, most of the world believed that the Earth was the center of the universe and that all planets and stars revolved around the Earth.

A famous mathematician named Copernicus developed a very different theory that said the sun, rather than the Earth, was at the center. Galileo's experiments, research, and inventions all supported Copernicus's theory.

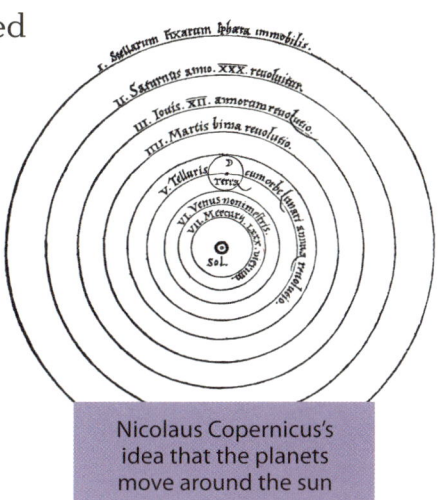

Nicolaus Copernicus's idea that the planets move around the sun

Statue of Nicolaus Copernicus in Warsaw, Poland

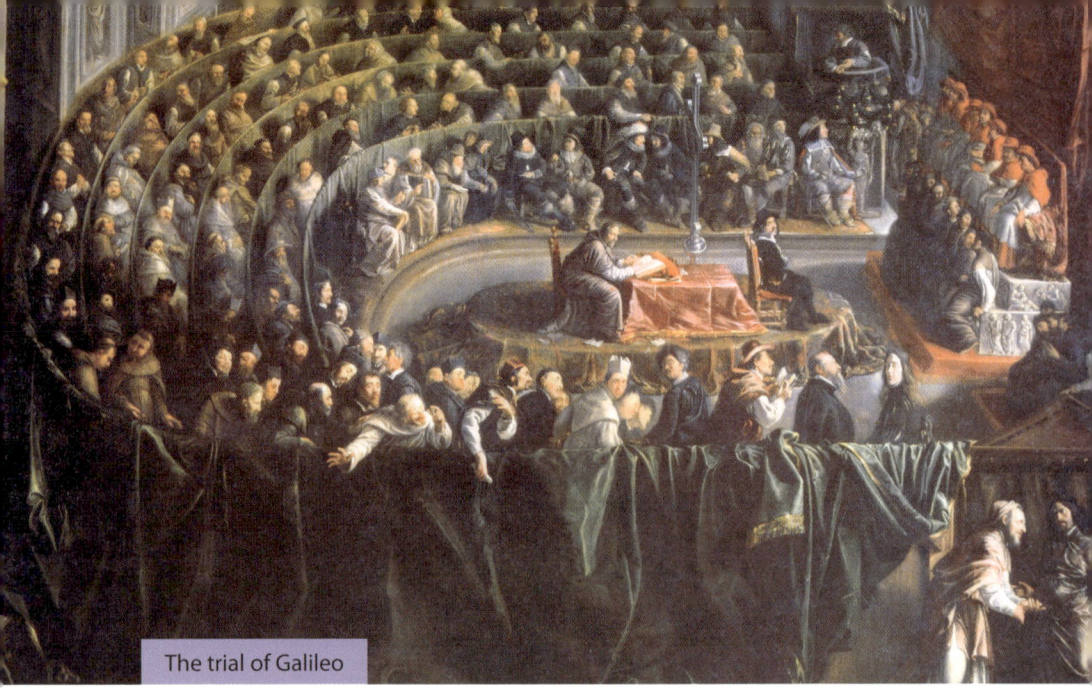

The trial of Galileo

Unfortunately for Galileo, the Catholic church strongly believed the Earth was the center of the universe and told him he must stop saying it was not. Galileo refused to lie and continued to publish more and more scientific papers.

Finally, the church arrested him and made him spend the last 10 years of his life under arrest in his house. He had no chance to talk anymore about his ideas on this topic.

Galileo Galilei looking at the wall of his prison cell, on which are scratched the words, "Still it moves."

Two New Sciences

Albert Einstein

Prison could not stop Galileo. At this time, Galileo wrote one of his most influential books ever called *Two New Sciences* which was smuggled out of Italy and printed in Holland. It established two completely new branches of science. The book was so good that hundreds of years later it received the praise of Albert Einstein.

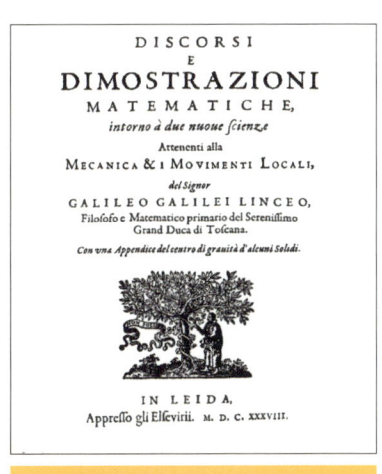

Galileo's book
Two New Sciences (1638)

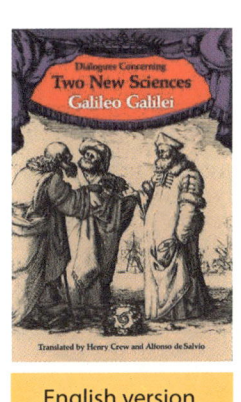

English version,
Two New Sciences

Improvements and Discoveries

Galileo had too many achievements in science and math to list them all. But here are a few highlights:

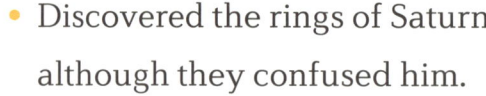

A ball following a curved path

- Showed that anything thrown on the Earth, such as a ball, follows a curved path.

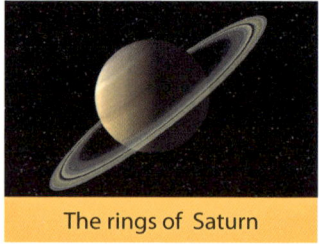

The rings of Saturn

- Discovered the rings of Saturn, although they confused him.

- Improved the design of telescopes so much that he made money building and selling them.

- Discovered that the Earth's moon has mountains.

The moon and the Earth

Galileo's amazing life and discoveries challenged people and society. He planted the seeds of the scientific method. And he gave us many scientific ideas. Galileo helped people understand the world and the universe around them.

Statue of Galileo in Padua, Italy

Tomb of Galileo, Santa Croce, Florence

Comprehension Questions

1. Galileo was born in…
   (a) a monastery in Italy.
   (b) Florence, Italy.
   (c) Pisa, Italy.
   (d) Padua, Italy.

2. As a child, he studied … with his father.
   (a) religion
   (b) math
   (c) science
   (d) music

3. Galileo…
   (a) lived 45 years ago.
   (b) never played music.
   (c) lived in a church.
   (d) did many experiments.

4. Some of his ideas were…
   (a) stolen from Einstein.
   (b) discovered by his brother.
   (c) not liked by the church.
   (d) slow.

5. Which of these did he NOT improve on or invent?
   (a) Pendulum clock
   (b) Telescope
   (c) Lute
   (d) Compass

6. He found out that objects fall…
   (a) at different speeds.
   (b) at the same speed.
   (c) on every planet.
   (d) slower on Saturn.

7. The scientific method is…
   (a) no longer used.
   (b) the normal way to do science now.
   (c) difficult for scientists.
   (d) weak science.

8. Galileo showed that…
   (a) the Earth goes around the sun.
   (b) the sun goes around the Earth.
   (c) the moon goes around the sun.
   (d) the Earth goes around the moon.

9. His book *Two New Sciences*…
   (a) was written by Einstein.
   (b) was written in the church.
   (c) was never published.
   (d) was meaningful and important.

10. Galileo was very interested in…
    (a) physics.
    (b) mathematics.
    (c) the scientific method.
    (d) All of the above

Glossary

- **compass** a device that shows the direction you are going

- **curved** bent in a shape like part of a circle

- **data** information or facts about something

- **era** a period of time in history that is special for a particular reason

- **experiment** a logical procedure to test an idea carefully

- **influential** having the power to change people or ideas

- **invention** something new that is made for the first time

- **lute** a musical instrument with strings

- **monastery** a place where monks (religious men) live

- **pendulum** a swinging weight on a stick or string that moves from one side to the other

- **physics** the scientific study of natural forces, such as heat, light, and energy

- **precise** exact

- **revolve** to move in a circle around a central point

- **smuggle** to take something into or out of a place secretly

- **telescope** a tube-shaped device used to see things far away

- **thermometer** a tube for measuring how hot or cold something is

- **universe** everything that exists in space, including the stars and planets

Image Credit/Pages

World History Timeline

This chart shows a rough overview of world history.
Some of the dates have been simplified.

World History Timeline

2900 BC	2800 BC	2700 BC	2600 BC	2500 BC

Narmer, Egyptian King
(c. 3000 BC)

Pyramids of Giza
(built c. 2550-2490 BC)

Cuneiform (c. 3000 BC-100 AD)

Old Egyptian Kingdom (c. 2686 BC)

2900 BC	2800 BC	2700 BC	2600 BC	2500 BC

← 5000 BC   Mesopotamia (Sumerians)

← 3100 BC   Early Dynastic Period of Egypt   Old Egyptian Kingdom

← 3650 BC   Minoan Civilization (Crete)

Early Bronze Age

2900 BC	2800 BC	2700 BC	2600 BC	2500 BC

2400 BC	2300 BC	2200 BC	2100 BC	2000 BC

Sahure, Egyptian King
(c. 2487-2475 BC)

Gudea of Lagash
(c. 2144-2124 BC)

Sargon the Great,
Akkadian King
(c. 2340-2284 BC)

Indus Valley
Civilization

Ur III Dynasty (c. 2112-2004 BC)

2400 BC	2300 BC	2200 BC	2100 BC	2000 BC

Xia Dynasty

Gutian Dynasty

Elam (Iran)

Akkadian Empire

Ur III Dynasty

Assyria (Early Period)

Middle Egyptian Kingdom

Minoan Civilization (Crete)

1st Intermediate
Period

Indus Valley Civilization (India)

2400 BC	2300 BC	2200 BC	2100 BC	2000 BC

World History Timeline

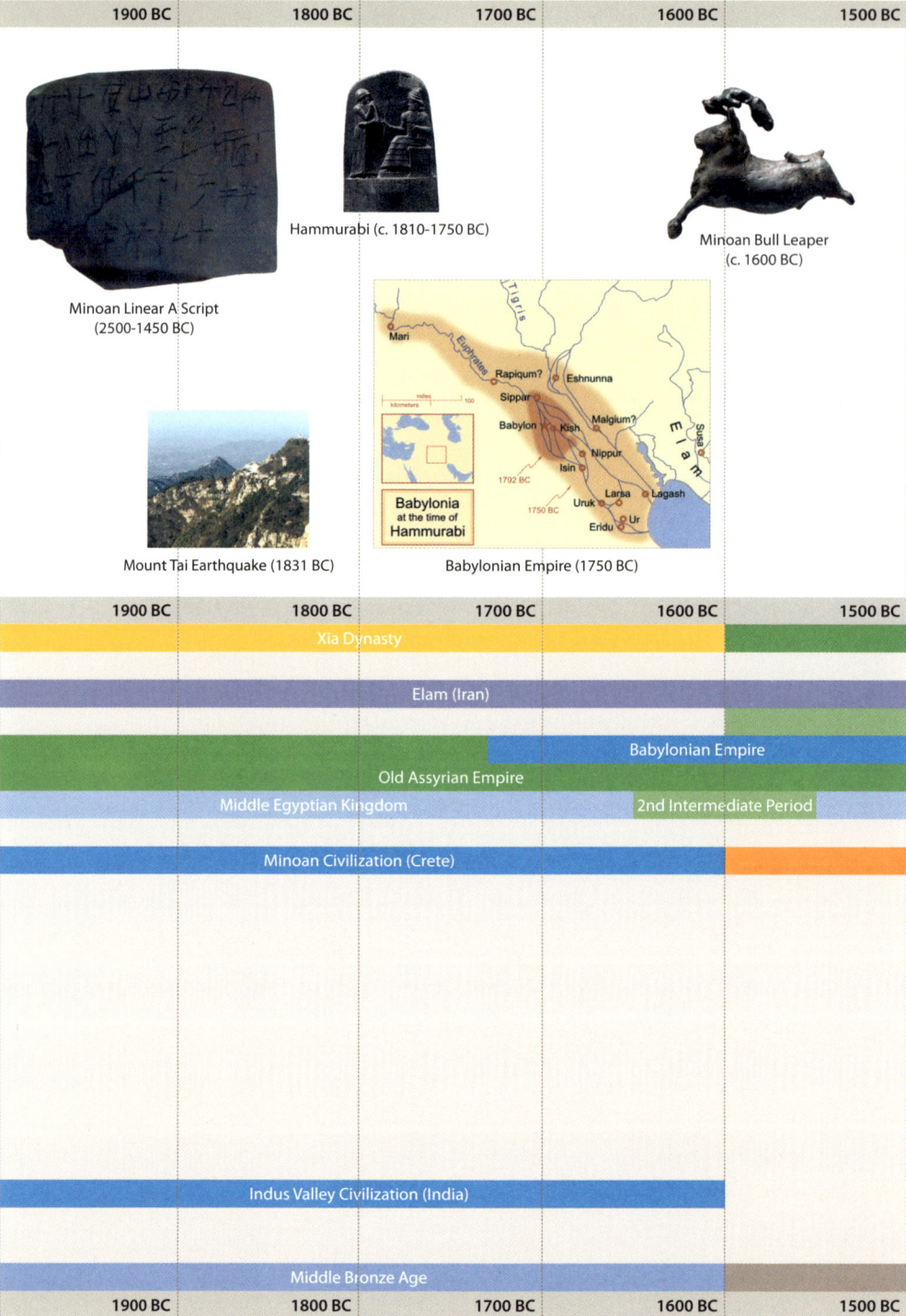

1900 BC	1800 BC	1700 BC	1600 BC	1500 BC

Hammurabi (c. 1810-1750 BC)

Minoan Bull Leaper
(c. 1600 BC)

Minoan Linear A Script
(2500-1450 BC)

Mount Tai Earthquake (1831 BC)

Babylonian Empire (1750 BC)

1900 BC	1800 BC	1700 BC	1600 BC	1500 BC

Xia Dynasty

Elam (Iran)

Babylonian Empire

Old Assyrian Empire

Middle Egyptian Kingdom

2nd Intermediate Period

Minoan Civilization (Crete)

Indus Valley Civilization (India)

Middle Bronze Age

1900 BC	1800 BC	1700 BC	1600 BC	1500 BC

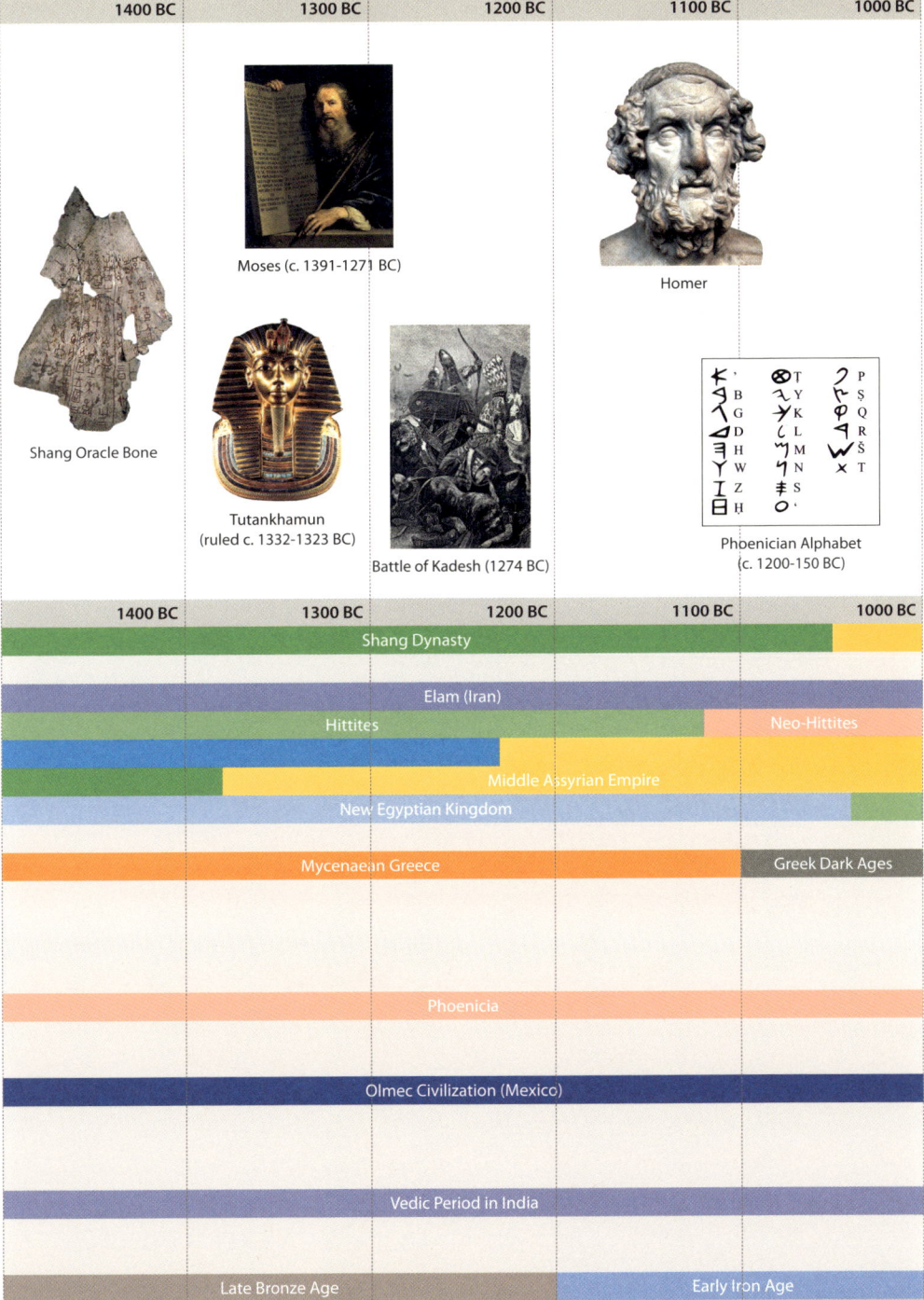

1400 BC	1300 BC	1200 BC	1100 BC	1000 BC

Moses (c. 1391-1271 BC)

Homer

Shang Oracle Bone

Tutankhamun
(ruled c. 1332-1323 BC)

Battle of Kadesh (1274 BC)

Phoenician Alphabet
(c. 1200-150 BC)

1400 BC	1300 BC	1200 BC	1100 BC	1000 BC

Shang Dynasty

Elam (Iran)

Hittites

Neo-Hittites

Middle Assyrian Empire

New Egyptian Kingdom

Mycenaean Greece

Greek Dark Ages

Phoenicia

Olmec Civilization (Mexico)

Vedic Period in India

Late Bronze Age

Early Iron Age

1400 BC	1300 BC	1200 BC	1100 BC	1000 BC

World History Timeline

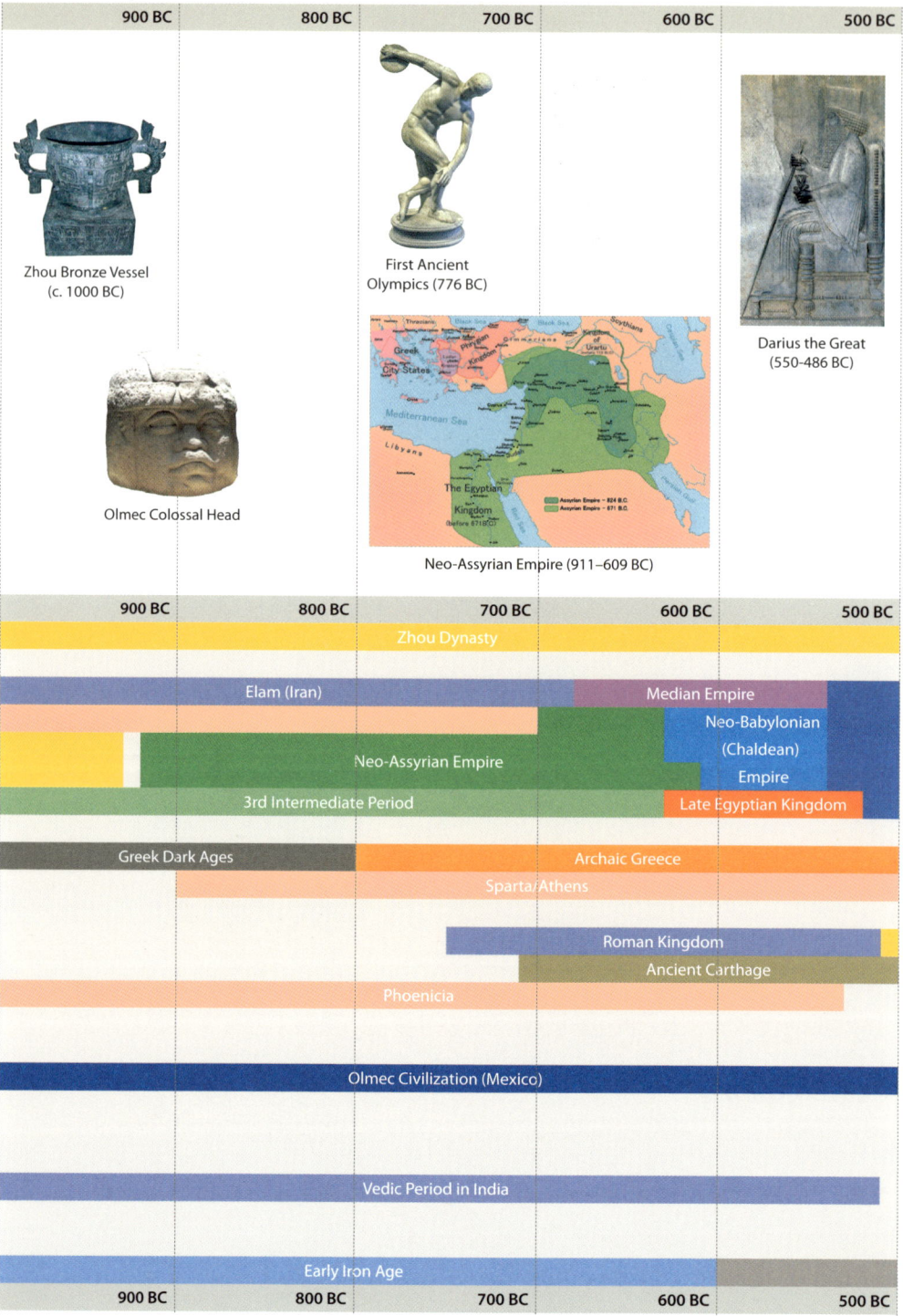

900 BC	800 BC	700 BC	600 BC	500 BC

Zhou Bronze Vessel
(c. 1000 BC)

First Ancient
Olympics (776 BC)

Olmec Colossal Head

Neo-Assyrian Empire (911–609 BC)

Darius the Great
(550–486 BC)

900 BC	800 BC	700 BC	600 BC	500 BC

Zhou Dynasty

Elam (Iran)

Median Empire

Neo-Assyrian Empire

Neo-Babylonian (Chaldean) Empire

3rd Intermediate Period

Late Egyptian Kingdom

Greek Dark Ages

Archaic Greece

Sparta/Athens

Roman Kingdom

Ancient Carthage

Phoenicia

Olmec Civilization (Mexico)

Vedic Period in India

Early Iron Age

900 BC	800 BC	700 BC	600 BC	500 BC

World History Timeline

400 BC	300 BC	200 BC	100 BC	0

Alexander the Great
(356-323 BC)

Julius Caesar
(100-44 BC)

Cleopatra
(69-30 BC)

Hannibal
(247-183 BC)

Battle of Salamis
(480 BC)

Seleucid Empire (312-63 BC)

Rossetta Stone
(created 196 BC)

400 BC	300 BC	200 BC	100 BC	0

Zhou Dynasty — Qin — Han Dynasty

Achaemenid (Persian) Empire

Alexander the Great

Parthian Empire

Seleucid Empire
Ptolemaic Kingdom
(Hellenistic Greece)

Classical Greece
Sparta/Athens

Roman Empire

Roman Republic

Roman Empire

Maurya Empire

Middle Iron Age

400 BC	300 BC	200 BC	100 BC	0

World History Timeline

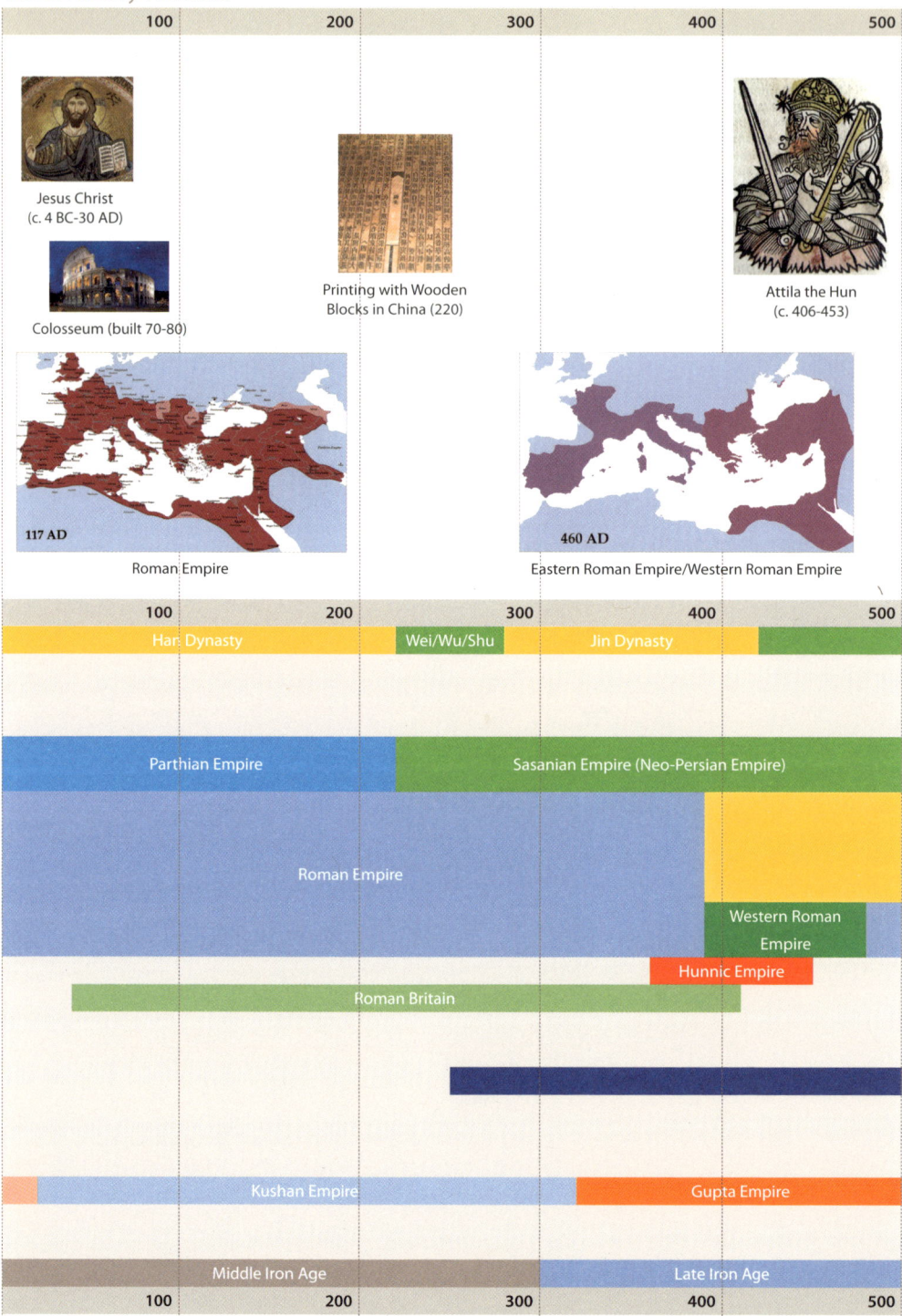

	100	200	300	400	500

Jesus Christ
(c. 4 BC-30 AD)

Colosseum (built 70-80)

Printing with Wooden
Blocks in China (220)

Attila the Hun
(c. 406-453)

117 AD

Roman Empire

460 AD

Eastern Roman Empire/Western Roman Empire

100	200	300	400	500

Han Dynasty

Wei/Wu/Shu

Jin Dynasty

Parthian Empire

Sasanian Empire (Neo-Persian Empire)

Roman Empire

Western Roman Empire

Hunnic Empire

Roman Britain

Kushan Empire

Gupta Empire

Middle Iron Age

Late Iron Age

100	200	300	400	500

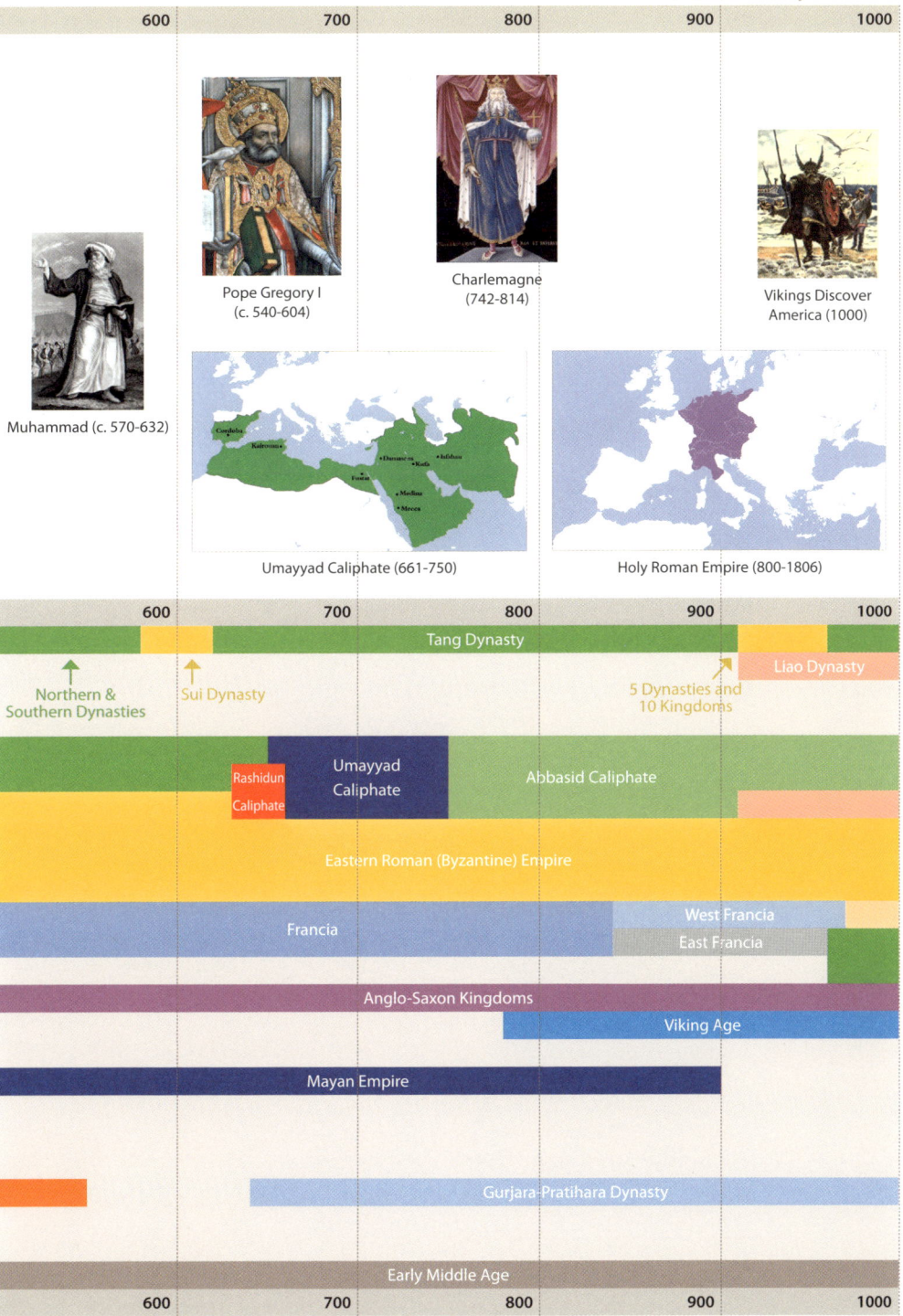

World History Timeline

600　　　700　　　800　　　900　　　1000

Muhammad (c. 570-632)

Pope Gregory I
(c. 540-604)

Charlemagne
(742-814)

Vikings Discover
America (1000)

Umayyad Caliphate (661-750)

Holy Roman Empire (800-1806)

600　　　700　　　800　　　900　　　1000

Tang Dynasty

Liao Dynasty

Northern &
Southern Dynasties

Sui Dynasty

5 Dynasties and
10 Kingdoms

Rashidun
Caliphate

Umayyad
Caliphate

Abbasid Caliphate

Eastern Roman (Byzantine) Empire

Francia

West Francia

East Francia

Anglo-Saxon Kingdoms

Viking Age

Mayan Empire

Gurjara-Pratihara Dynasty

Early Middle Age

600　　　700　　　800　　　900　　　1000

World History Timeline

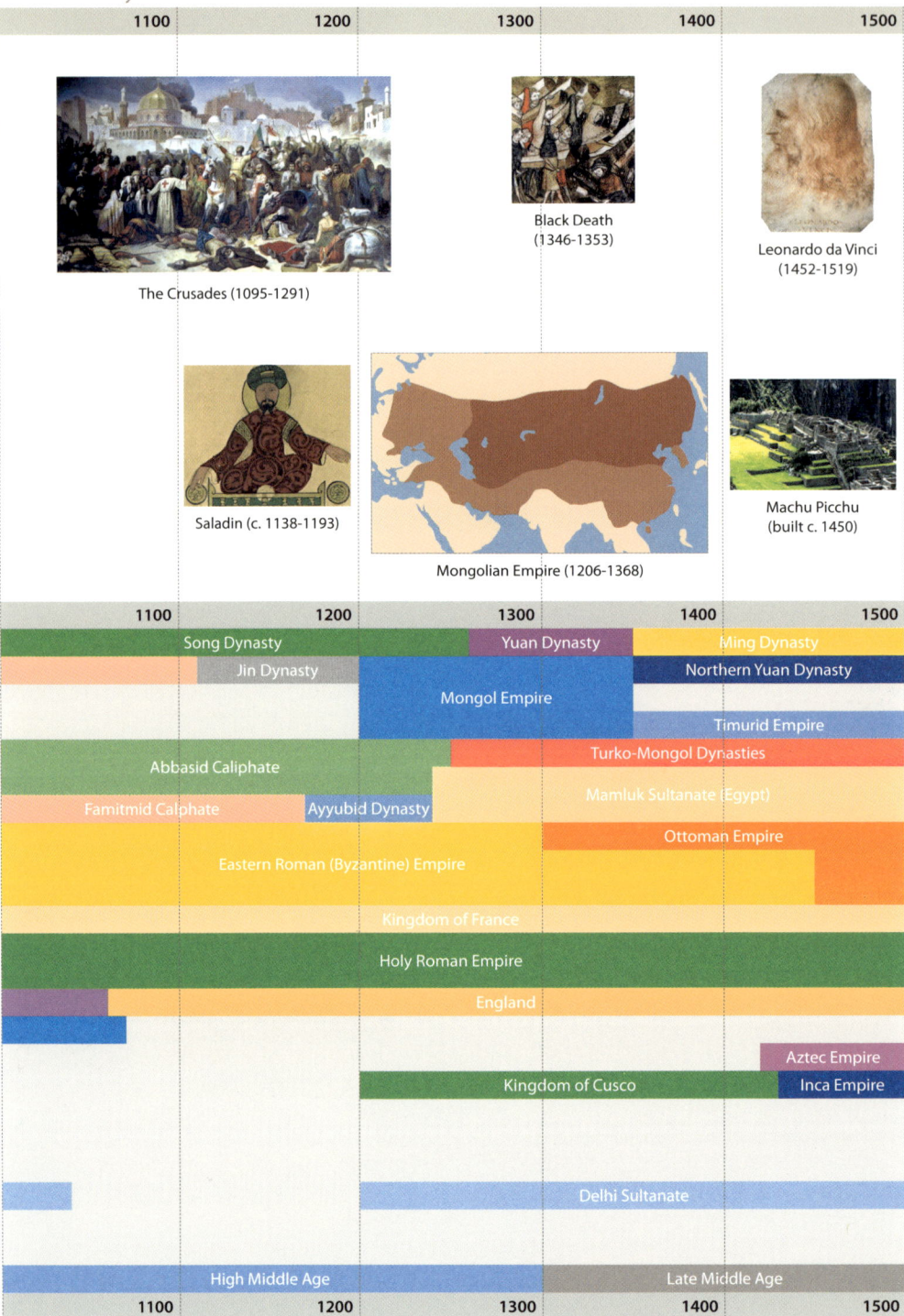

The Crusades (1095-1291)

Black Death (1346-1353)

Leonardo da Vinci (1452-1519)

Saladin (c. 1138-1193)

Mongolian Empire (1206-1368)

Machu Picchu (built c. 1450)

| 1100 | 1200 | 1300 | 1400 | 1500 |

Song Dynasty

Yuan Dynasty

Ming Dynasty

Jin Dynasty

Northern Yuan Dynasty

Mongol Empire

Timurid Empire

Abbasid Caliphate

Turko-Mongol Dynasties

Famitmid Calphate

Ayyubid Dynasty

Mamluk Sultanate (Egypt)

Ottoman Empire

Eastern Roman (Byzantine) Empire

Kingdom of France

Holy Roman Empire

England

Aztec Empire

Kingdom of Cusco

Inca Empire

Delhi Sultanate

High Middle Age

Late Middle Age

| 1100 | 1200 | 1300 | 1400 | 1500 |